Ancient Rome

Fiona Macdonald
Consultant: Richard Tames

Miles Kelly
PUBLISHING

First published in 2002 by
Miles Kelly Publishing Ltd
Bardfield Centre, Great Bardfield, Essex, CM7 4SL

Some material in this book can also be found in *100 Things You Should Know About Ancient Rome.*

Editor: Amanda Learmonth

Design: Debbie Meekcoms

Index: Lynn Bresler

Art Director: Clare Sleven

Editorial Director: Paula Borton

British Library Cataloguing-in-Publication Data
A catalogue record for this book is available from the British Library

ISBN 1-84236-104-X

Printed in Hong Kong

www.mileskelly.net
info@mileskelly.net

ACKNOWLEDGEMENTS

The Publishers would like to thank the following artists who have contributed to this book:

Brett Brecon, Jim Channell, Terry Gabbey (AFA), Luigi Galante (Studio Galante), John James (Temple Rogers), Richard Hook (Linden Artists Ltd.), Kevin Maddison, Rob Sheffield, Rudi Vizi, Mike White (Temple Rogers)

Computer-generated cartoons by James Evans

Contents

Rome and its empire

The city of Rome, in Italy, was once the centre of a great empire.
An empire is made up of many different countries governed by a single ruler. Rome ruled over 50 million people around the world. The city was busy, noisy and exciting, with many beautiful buildings.

Temple

Market-place

4

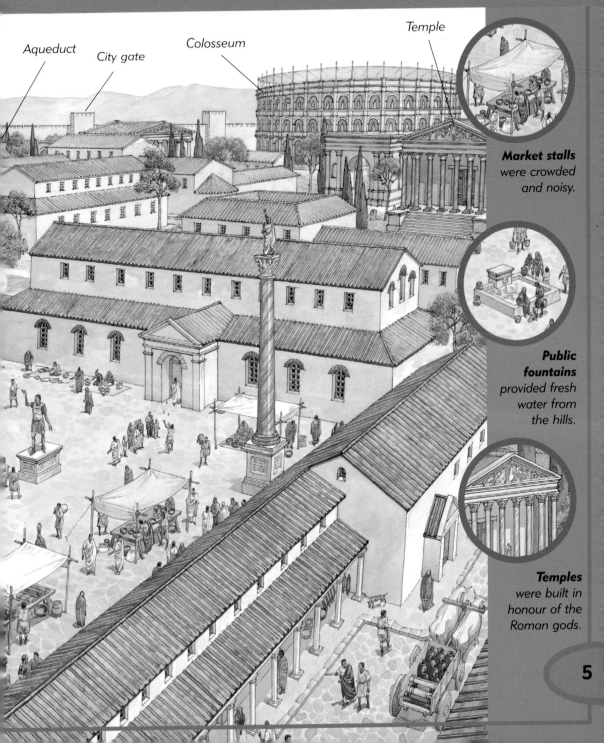

Aqueduct

City gate

Colosseum

Temple

Market stalls were crowded and noisy.

Public fountains provided fresh water from the hills.

Temples were built in honour of the Roman gods.

5

The people of Rome

By around AD300, Rome was the largest city in the world. Over a million people lived there. The government was run by nobles and knights who were usually very rich. Ordinary citizens, called Plebeians, were quite poor but they could vote and serve in the army. Slaves were not citizens. They could not leave their owners and had no rights.

▼ The Forum of Rome was the heart of the city. People came here to chat with their friends or have business meetings.

City guards protected Rome from outside attackers.

Senators were important government leaders.

Julius's fun facts!

Roman engineers also designed public lavatories. These lavatories were convenient, but not private. Users sat on rows of seats, side by side!

Family life

To the Romans, a 'family' meant all the people living and working together in the same household. So families included many different slaves and servants, as well as a husband and wife and their children.

Test your memory!

1. How many people did Rome rule around the world?

2. What is the name for lots of countries that are governed by a single ruler?

3. How many people lived in Rome by AD300?

4. What is the Roman name for ordinary people?

1. over 50 million 2. empire 3. over a million 4. Plebeians

A Roman father was in charge of the whole family.

Roman girls could marry from the age of 12.

Family pets included cats, dogs and even deer!

Going shopping

Rome housed the world's first shopping mall. It was called Trajan's market, and was built on five different levels on the slopes of the Quirinal Hill in the centre of Rome. It contained over 150 different shops together with a large main hall.

Shop like the Romans!

Imagine you are a Roman going shopping in Trajan's market – what will you buy and from which shop? Look at the two lists below. Try to match the shop on the left with the correct item of shopping on the right:

1. Take-away shop
2. Butchers
3. Fishmongers
4. Bakers

a. Honey cakes
b. Cabbage soup
c. Wild pig
d. Sea urchin

1 and b, 2 and c, 3 and d, 4 and a

Romans liked a bargain. They haggled to get a cheaper price.

Roman take-aways served up soup, lentils or beans.

Pottery jars were used for carrying fish sauce or wine.

Eating and drinking

Most Romans ate very little during the day.
They had bread and water for breakfast and a
light snack of bread, cheese or fruit around
midday. They ate their main meal at about 4pm.
In rich people's homes, a meal would have three
separate courses. Poor people ate much simpler
foods, such as lentil soup and barley porridge.

Real Roman Food

Try this real Roman recipe!
PEAR MOUSSE

You will need: 1 kg pears, peeled and cored, 6 eggs beaten, 4 tblsp honey, a little bit of oil, $\frac{1}{2}$ tsp cumin and some ground pepper to taste.

··

1. Mash the pears together with the pepper, cumin, honey and a bit of oil. Ask an adult to help.
2. Add the beaten eggs and put into a casserole.
3. Cook for around 30 minutes in a moderate oven.
4. Serve with a little bit of pepper sprinkled on top.

Banquet food included roast meats, wine and dates.

Grapes and olives were popular Roman food.

A silver jug like this was used by rich people for serving wine.

Going to school

Roman boys learnt three main subjects, reading, maths – and public speaking!
Boys needed all three skills for their future careers. There were no newspapers or television, so important people such as politicians had to make speeches in public. Boys went to school from around seven years old and left aged 16. Most Roman girls did not go to school. They stayed at home where they learned how to look after the house.

Learn some Roman words!

The Romans spoke a language called **Latin**.
It forms the basis of many languages today, and below you can learn some Latin for yourself!
liber = book   **epistola** = letter
biblioteca = library   **vellum** = calfskin
stylus = writing stick
(used with wax tablets)
librarii = slaves who work in a library
grammaticus = schoolmaster
paedagogus = private tutor

▼ *Roman schoolboys practise reading with their slave schoolmaster.*

Wax tablet
Wax could be smoothed over and used again.

Pens (left) and stylus (right)
A stylus was used with the wax tablet.

Ink pot
Roman ink was made of soot, vinegar and sticky gum!

Roman fashion

Romans clothes were different depending on how important you were. Ordinary men and women wore plain white togas. Rich men and women wore robes made of smooth, fine-quality wool and silk. Ordinary people's clothes were much rougher.

Dress like a Roman!

You can wear your very own toga – follow the instructions below!

1  First ask an adult for a blanket or a sheet. White is best, like the Romans.

2 Drape your sheet over your left shoulder. Now pass the rest behind your back.

3 Pull the sheet across your front, so that you're wrapped up in it. You're almost a Roman now!

4 Finally, drape the last end over your right hand and there you have it, a Roman toga!

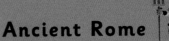

A Roman comb was made of ivory, bone or wood.

Roman shoes had studs to stop them wearing down too quickly.

olive oil

Bark and flowers to make perfume

olives

Saffron for make-up

perfume bottle

Ash to darken eyelids

Roman hairstyles took a long time to fix!

▲ The Romans used olive oil to soften their skins, and perfume to scent their bodies.

A trip to the baths

Romans baths were more than a place to get clean. They were also places to relax, meet friends and get fit. Visitors could take part in sports, such as wrestling, do exercises, have a massage or a haircut. They could buy scented oils and perfumes, read a book or eat a snack. Or they could admire works of art in the baths' own sculpture gallery!

▶ There were public baths in most districts of Rome. They were built by Roman emperors or rich families.

Julius's fun facts!

Although the Romans liked bathing, they only visited the baths once in every nine days!

A massage was the perfect way to relax.

Men's baths were separate from the women's.

Washing was done without soap. Romans scraped the dirt off instead!

19

Having fun

▼ All the parts in Roman plays were played by men.

The Romans liked music and dancing. They played instruments such as pipes, cymbals and horns. The Romans also enjoyed going to the theatre to see comedies. They also invented mime, a story told without words through gestures and dance.

Buskers
played in the
streets or
could be hired
for parties.

Masks were
often worn by
actors to help
identify the
characters.

Julius's fun facts!

Roman actors
were so popular
that women
couldn't sit
near the stage,
in case they tried to
arrange a date with
one of the stars!

Gladiator games

Gladiator fights were popular with the Romans. People admired gladiators for their strength, bravery and skill. But gladiators' lives were short and their deaths were horrible. They were sent to the arena to fight until they died. Most did even not choose to fight. They were either criminals or prisoners-of-war.

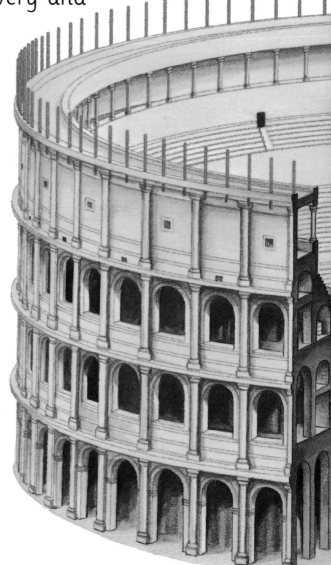

▶ The Colosseum was the largest amphitheatre (circular building) in the Roman empire.

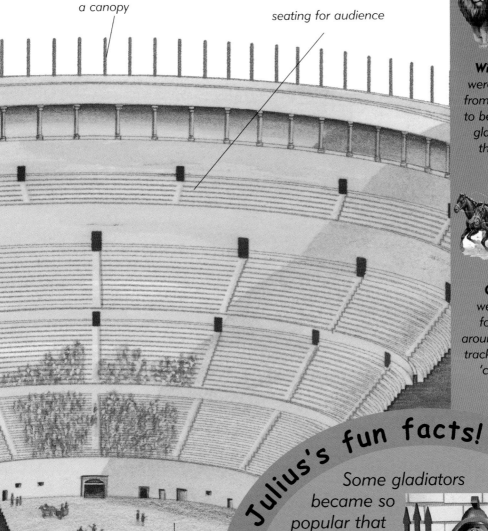

poles to support
a canopy

seating for audience

tunnels for prisoners
and beasts

arena

Wild beasts were brought from far away to be killed by gladiators in the arenas.

Chariots were used for racing around race-tracks called 'circuses'.

Julius's fun facts!

Some gladiators became so popular that people wrote graffiti about them on the walls of buildings around Rome!

Rulers of Rome

▼ The republic of Rome was governed by the Senate. This was a room where groups of senators met to make new laws and discuss government plans.

Rome was once ruled by kings. In 509BC the last king, Tarquin the Proud, was overthrown. Rome then became a republic, a state without a king. After many years of civil war, an army general called Octavian took power, bringing peace and better laws to Rome. He took a new name, 'Augustus', and became the first emperor of Rome.

▼ The 'basilica', or town hall, was used as a lawcourt and for other business meetings.

Julius Caesar was a general who was killed when he became too powerful.

Octavian became the first emperor of Rome in 27BC.

A lawyer, called an 'advocatus', helped to prove an accused person was innocent

...erson accused of committing a crime ...s brought to the town hall for trial

Julius's fun facts!

The mad Emperor Nero was said to have laughed and played music while watching a terrible fire destroy part of Rome.

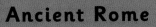

In the army

Being a soldier was a very good career, if you did not get killed! Roman soldiers were well paid and well cared for. The empire needed troops to defend its land against enemy attack. A soldier received good training in battle skills. When he retired after 20 or 25 years of service, he was given money or land to help him start a business.

Julius's fun facts!

Roman soldiers kept warm in cold countries by wearing woolly underpants beneath their tunics!

▶ Soldiers used their shields to make a protective shell called a 'testudo', or tortoise.

Roman cavalry guarded the foot-soldiers during battle.

A Roman foot-soldier had to carry a heavy pack.

A Gladius was a short sword worn on the right.

27

A country farm

Rome relied on farmers.
Most people in Roman
times lived in the countryside
and worked on farms.
Farmers produced food
for city-dwellers. Food
was grown on big estates
by teams of slaves, and
on small peasant
farms where families
worked together.

Test your memory!

The picture below shows people
pressing olives to make oil. Can
you remember something the
Romans used olive oil for?

Softening the skin, perfume

Threshing wheat
Donkeys ground the grain to be made into flour.

Beehives
Bees were kept to produce honey.

Treading grapes
Workers pressed grapes with their bare feet to make wine.

Life as a slave

Roman people were not all equal. The biggest difference between people was whether they were slaves or free. Free-born people had rights by law, for example, to find their own work or to travel around. But slaves had hardly any rights at all. They belonged to their owners just like dogs or horses.

Julius's fun facts!

Slaves were sometimes set free by dying owners who didn't want their slaves to pass to a new owner who might be cruel.

Ancient Rome

▼ *Slaves were bought and sold at slave-markets like this one.*

Rich Romans *were carried round by slaves in 'litters', or curtained beds.*

Slaves *were paraded before the citizens to be bought.*

A slave-trader *made his living from buying and selling slaves.*

31

Building Rome

The Romans invented many new building materials and techniques. They were the first to use concrete, which was much cheaper and easier to use than solid building stone, and they worked out how to build arches to create tall, strong doorways. They even invented special pumps that pushed water uphill.

▶ The Romans were amazing builders and architects. Their roads and many of their buildings have lasted over 2000 years.

Domes
were designed
for the roofs of
large buildings.

Aqueducts
carried fresh
water from
far-away hills
to the city.

Julius's fun facts!

Our word
'plumber' comes
from 'plumbum',
the Latin word for
lead. The same
word is used for a
'plumb-line', still
in use today.

Gods and goddesses

The Romans worshipped many different gods and goddesses. There was a god for almost everything, from love and war to wild animals and people's homes. The Roman emperor offered sacrifices to the gods who protected Rome. Ordinary Roman people also made offerings to the gods, leaving food, wine and incense in front of a shrine in their house.

8   9

7

6

Gods and Goddesses

1. Mars, god of war.
2. Venus, goddess of love.
3. Minerva, goddess of war.
4. Diana, goddess of the moon and hunting.
5. Pan, god of the mountain-side, pastures, sheep and goats.
6. Neptune, god of the sea.
7. Mercury, messenger of the gods.
8. Jupiter, king of the gods.
9. Juno, queen of the gods.

Curse tablet
People wrote to the gods asking them to harm someone they didn't like!

Family shrine
This was like a mini church inside people's homes.

Julius's fun facts!

After an animal had been sacrificed to the gods, a priest, called a 'haruspex', examined its liver. If it was diseased, bad luck was on the way!

Roman roads

Rome's first main road was built in 312BC.
All roads led to Rome. The city was at the centre of a network of roads that stretched for over 85,000 kilometres. They had been built to link far-away parts of the empire to Rome, so that Roman armies or government leaders could travel more easily. To make travel as quick as possible, roads were built in straight lines, taking the shortest route.

route accurately marked out

large surface slabs

drainage ditch

A road engineer used a 'grome' to measure straight lines.

Stone slabs were carefully fitted together for a smooth road surface.

Julius's fun facts!

The Romans would often consult a fortune-teller or a priest before setting out on a long journey.

Clues to the past

A large amount of evidence has survived to tell us about Roman times. Archaeologists, who study the remains of the past, have dug up what is left of many Roman buildings, such as palaces, forts and ordinary family homes. They have also found Roman works of art and objects used by Romans in their daily lives.

Test your memory!

1. Who was the king of the Roman gods?
2. What is the proper name for a mini church in someone's house?
3. When was Rome's first road built?
4. What is the proper name for a curtained bed?

1. Jupiter 2. a shrine 3. 312BC 4. a litter

Roman coins show important people of the time, such as the emperor.

Roman pots tell us how people stored their food.

Statues can give us an idea what the Romans looked like.

An archaeologist digs into the ground to find clues about the past.

Index